AUDIO ACCESS INCLUDED

The Easy
UKULELE
CHORD SOLO
SONGBOOK

T0061500

PLAYBACK+
Speed • Pitch • Balance • Loop

To access audio visit:
www.halleonard.com/mylibrary

"Enter Code"
5888-3037-8301-9917

ISBN 978-1-5400-3289-8

HAL•LEONARD®

Visit Hal Leonard Online at
www.halleonard.com

Contact us:
Hal Leonard
7777 West Bluemound Road
Milwaukee, WI 53213
Email: info@halleonard.com

In Europe, contact:
Hal Leonard Europe Limited
42 Wigmore Street
Marylebone, London, W1U 2RN
Email: info@halleonardeurope.com

In Australia, contact:
Hal Leonard Australia Pty. Ltd.
4 Lentara Court
Cheltenham, Victoria, 3192 Australia
Email: info@halleonard.com.au

Africa

Words and Music by David Paich and Jeff Porcaro

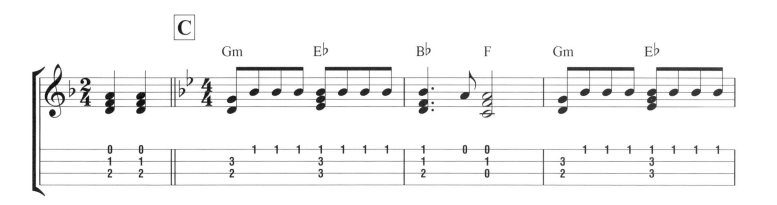

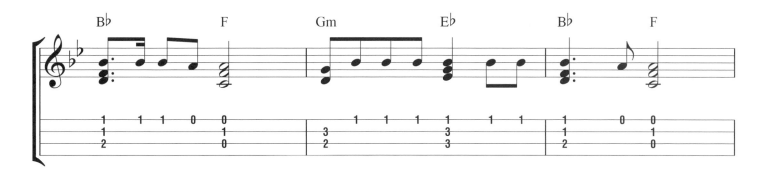

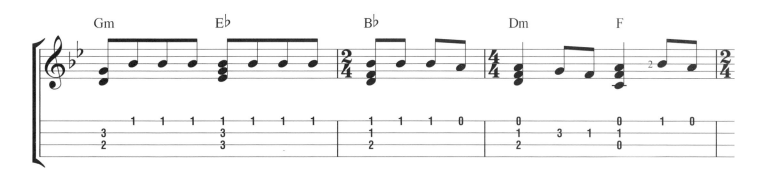

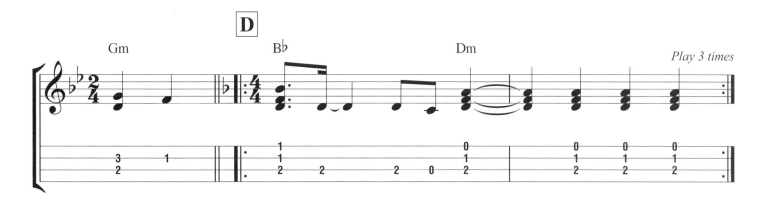

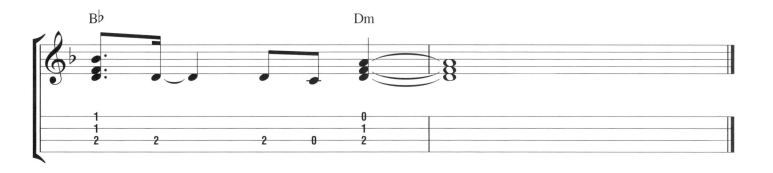

American Pie

Words and Music by Don McLean

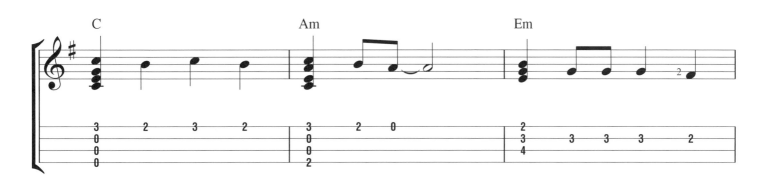

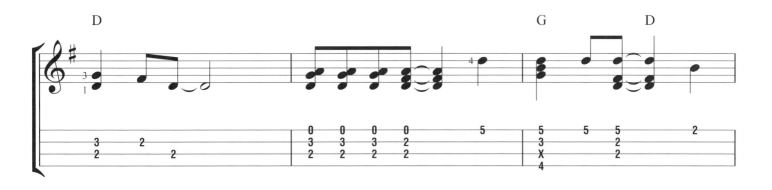

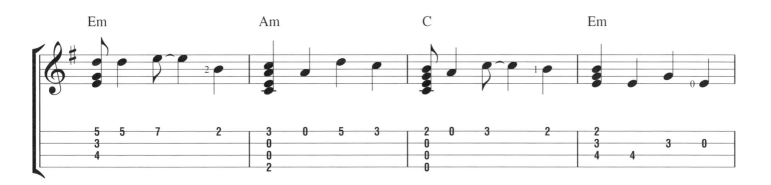

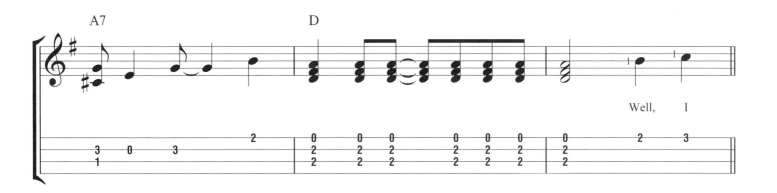

Well, I

C

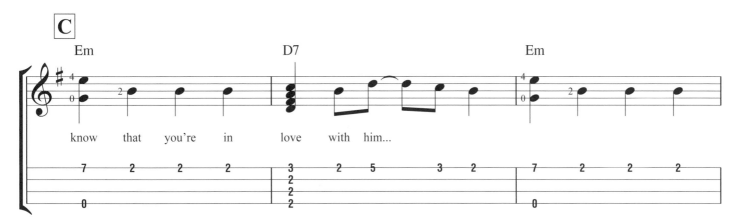

know that you're in love with him...

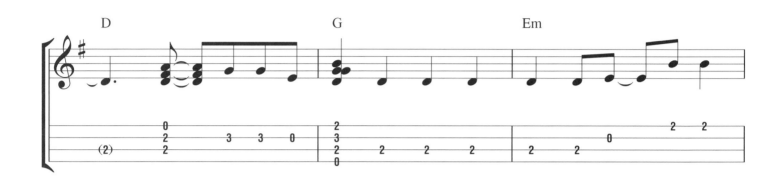

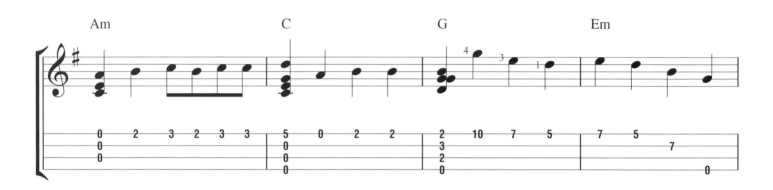

D.S. al Coda

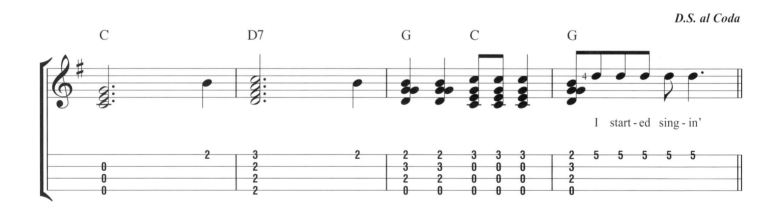

I start-ed sing-in'

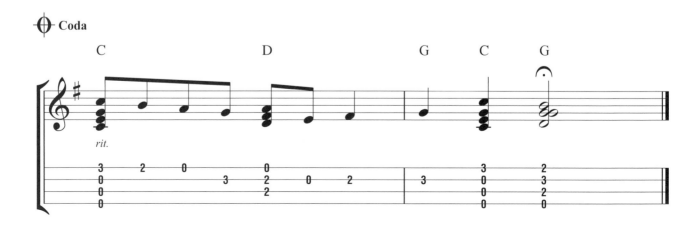

6

Don't Stop Believin'

Words and Music by Steve Perry, Neal Schon and Jonathan Cain

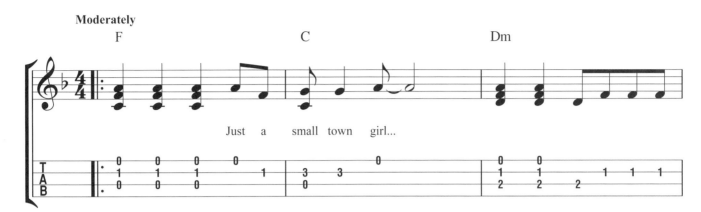

Just a small town girl...

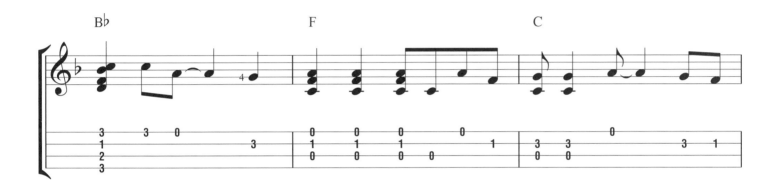

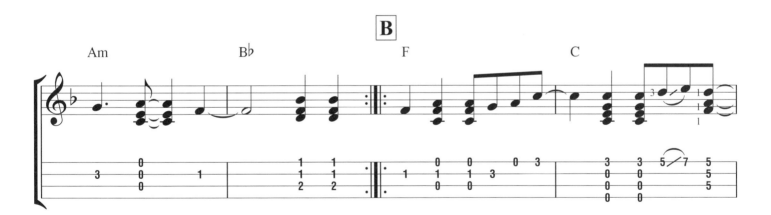

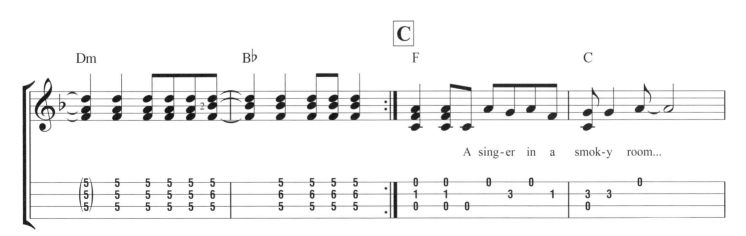

A sing-er in a smok-y room...

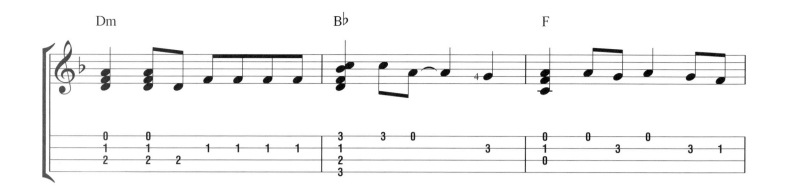

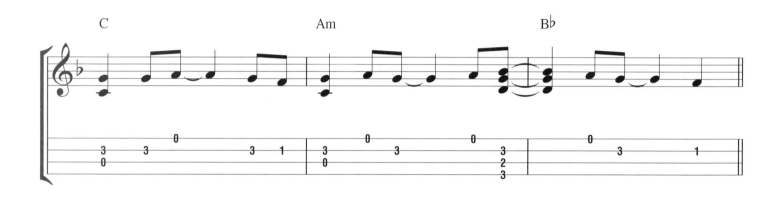

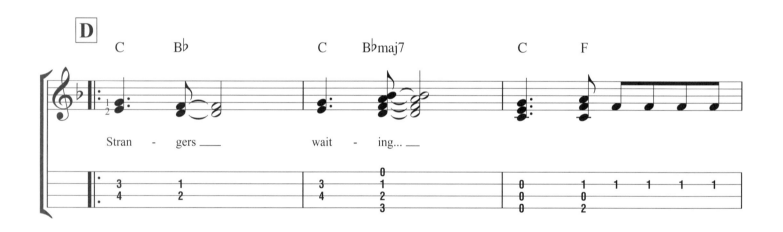

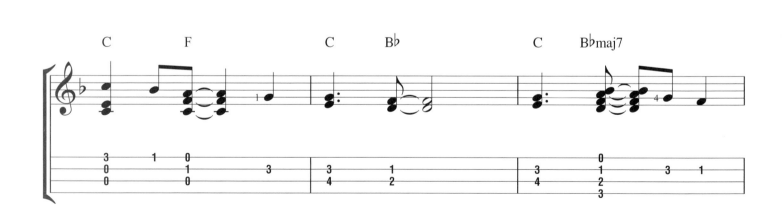

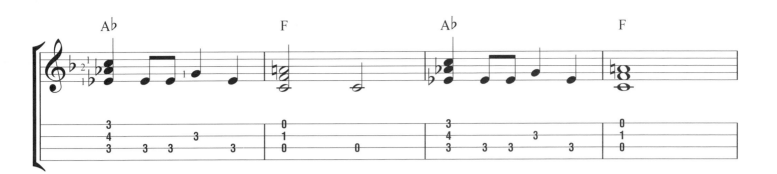

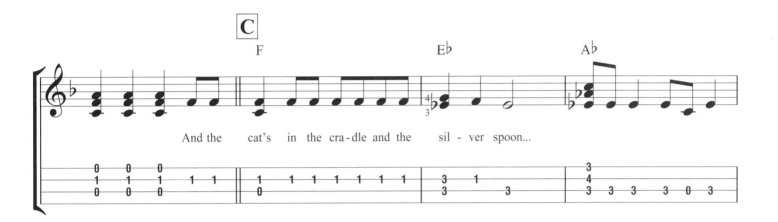

And the   cat's   in the cra-dle and the   sil - ver spoon...

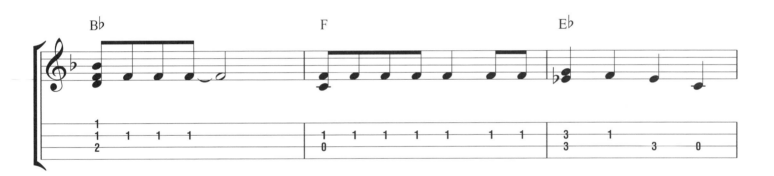

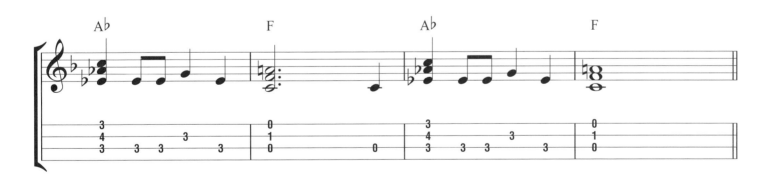

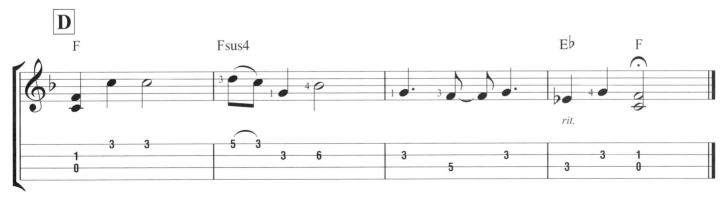

Every Breath You Take

Music and Lyrics by Sting

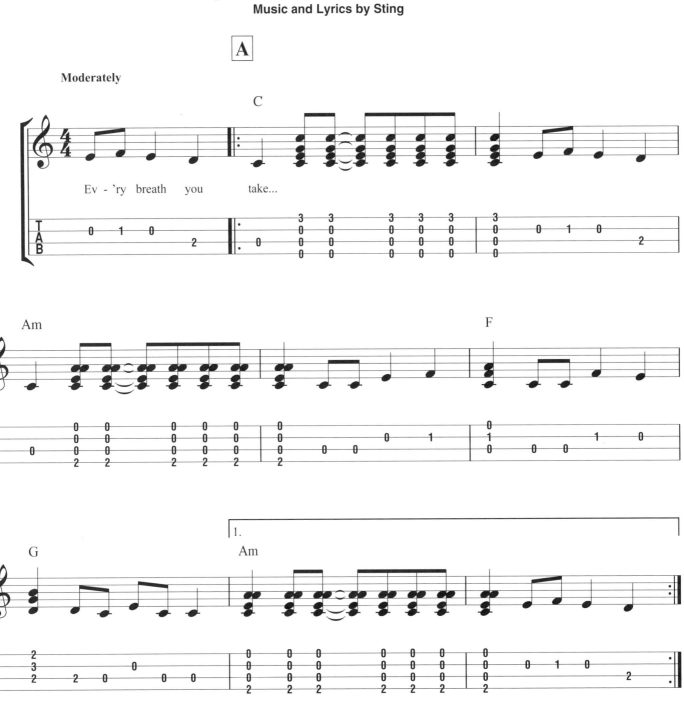

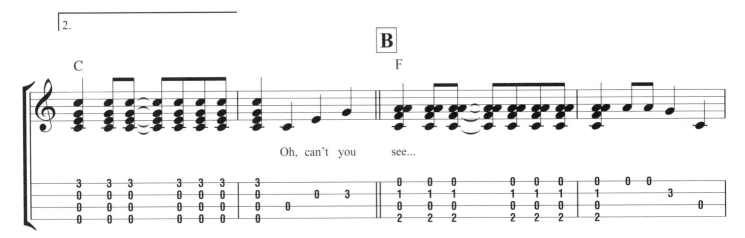

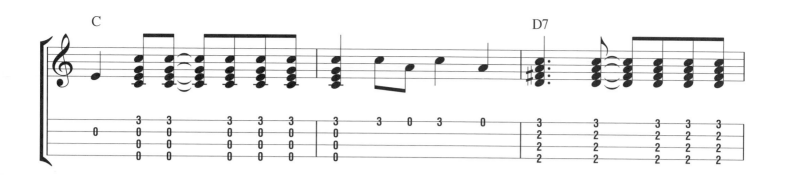

C

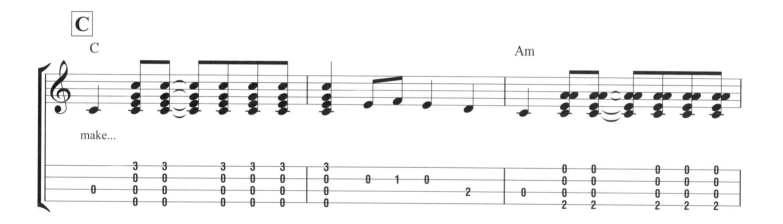

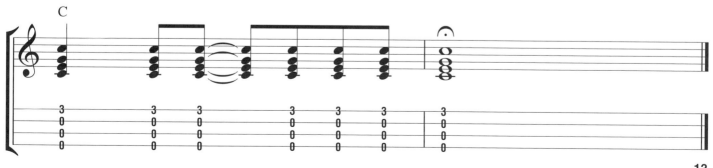

Good Riddance
(Time of Your Life)

Words by Billie Joe
Music by Green Day

An - oth - er   turn - ing point...

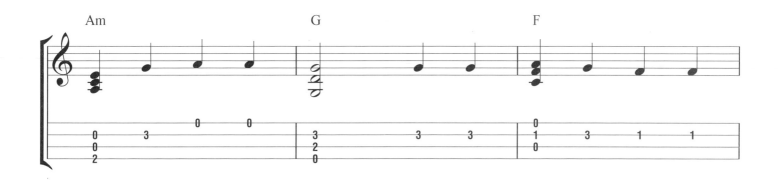

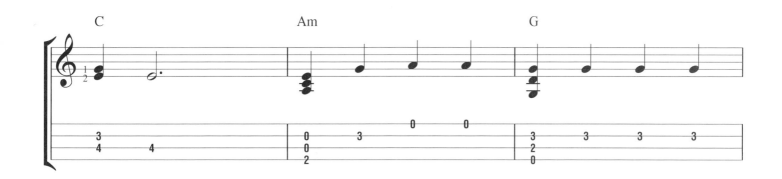

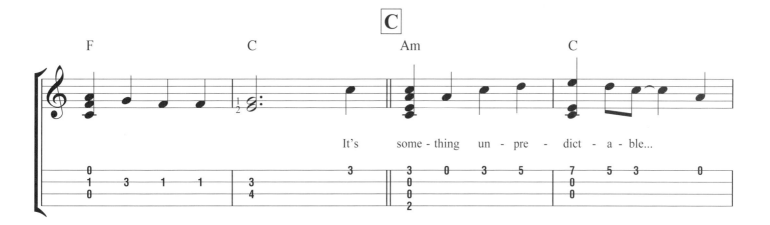

It's   some - thing   un - pre - dict - a - ble...

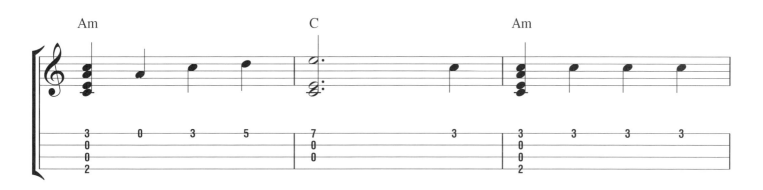

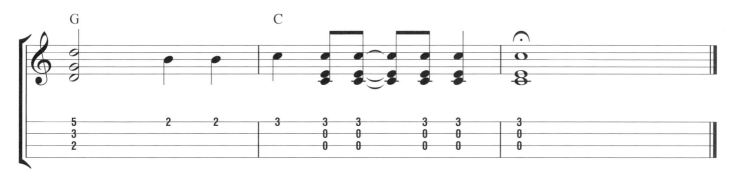

Heart of Glass

Words and Music by Deborah Harry and Chris Stein

Once I had a love ___ and it was a gas...

In be-tween...

Help!

Words and Music by John Lennon and Paul McCartney

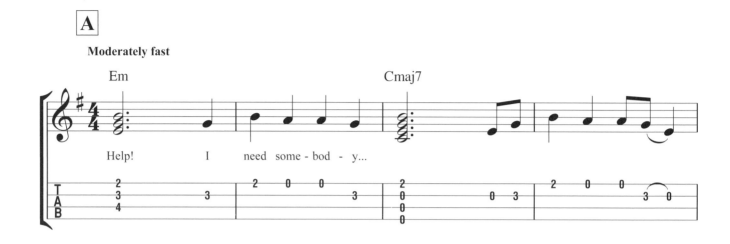

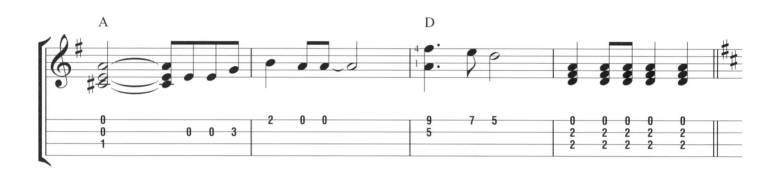

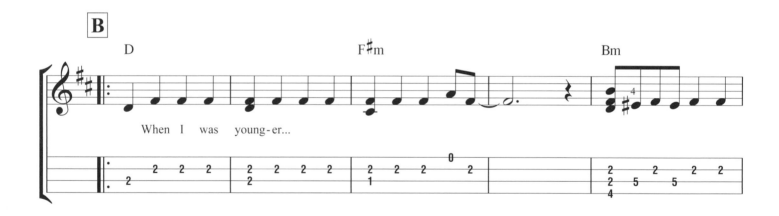

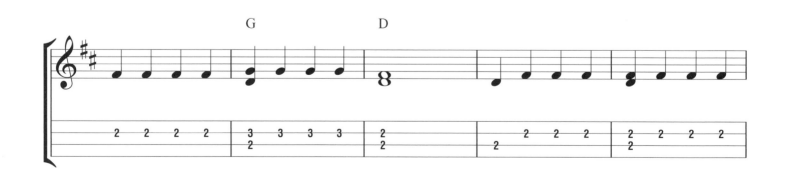

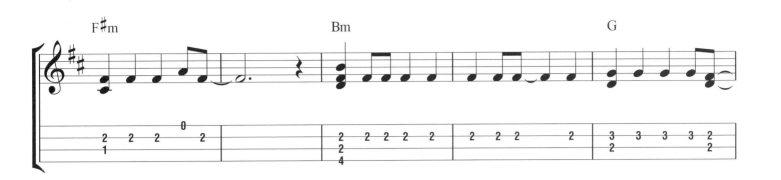

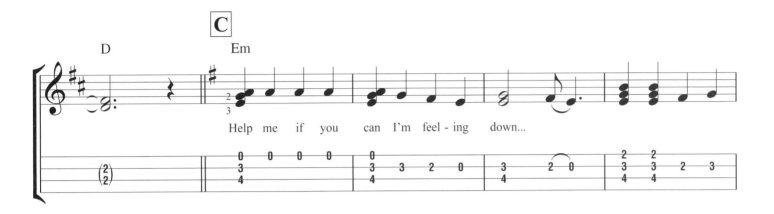

Help me if you can I'm feel-ing down...

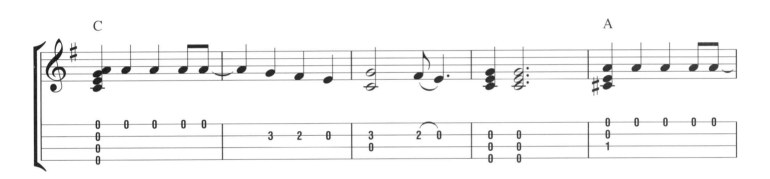

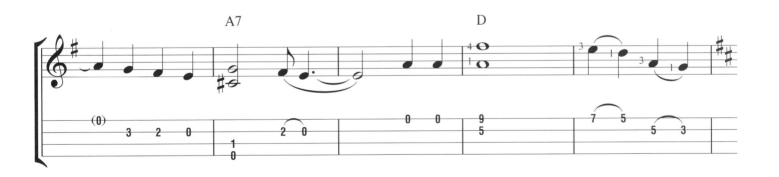

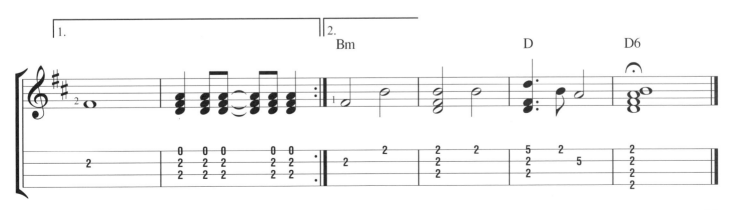

I Can See Clearly Now

Words and Music by Johnny Nash

I can see clear - ly now...

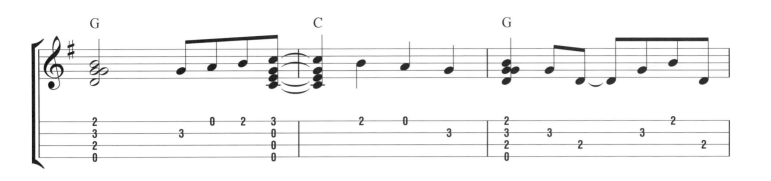

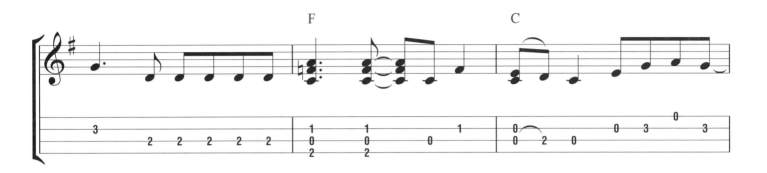

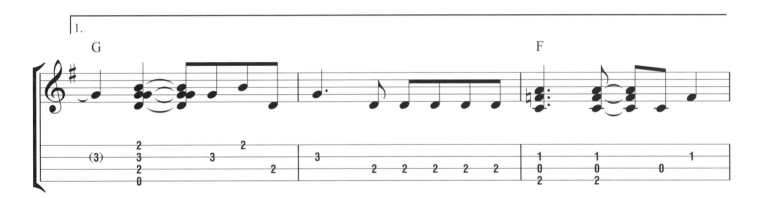

Look all a-round...

D.S. al Coda
(take 1st ending)

Coda

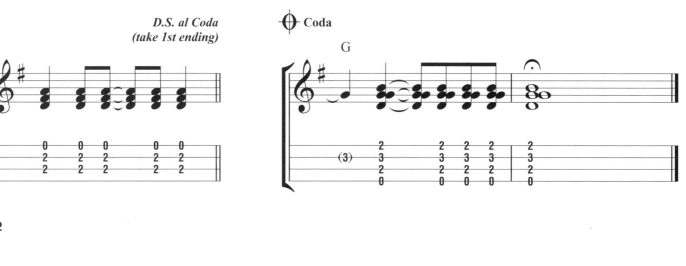

Sweet Caroline

Words and Music by Neil Diamond

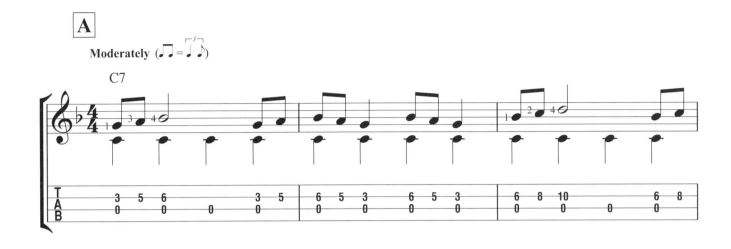

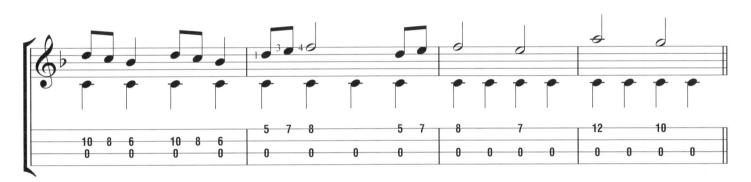

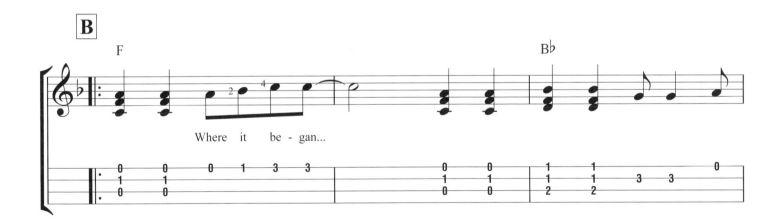

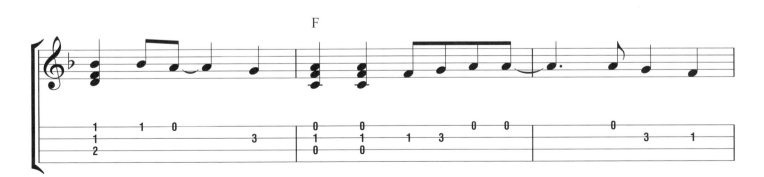

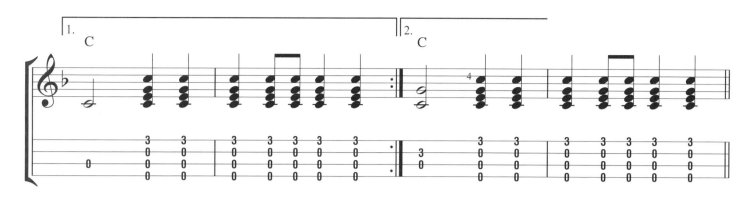

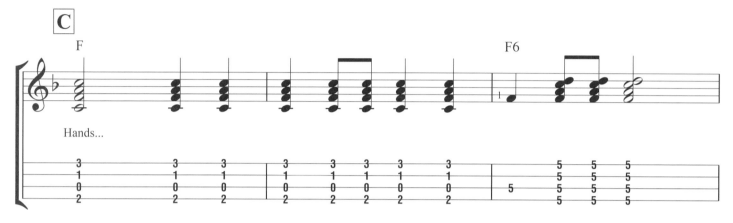

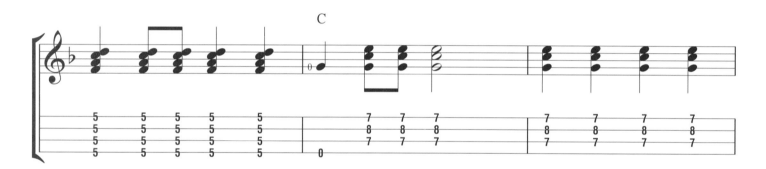

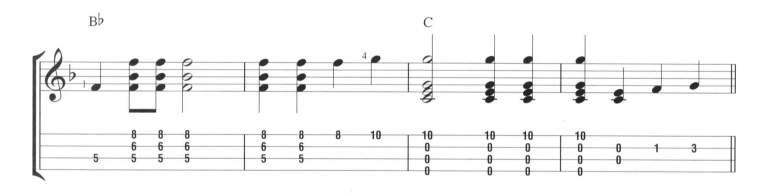

Lean on Me

Words and Music by Bill Withers

Some - times in our lives...

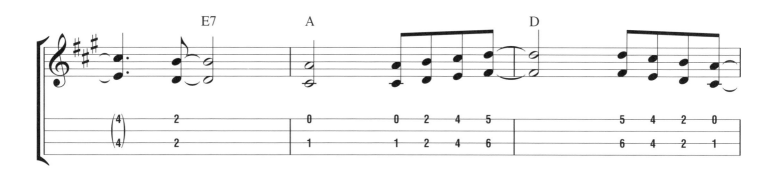

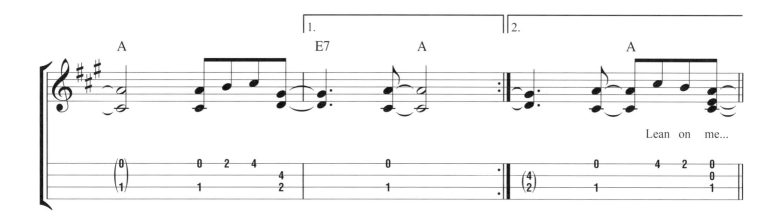

Lean on me...

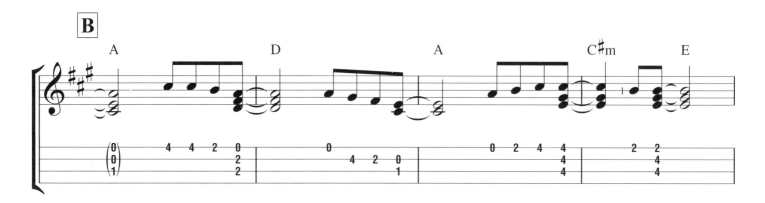

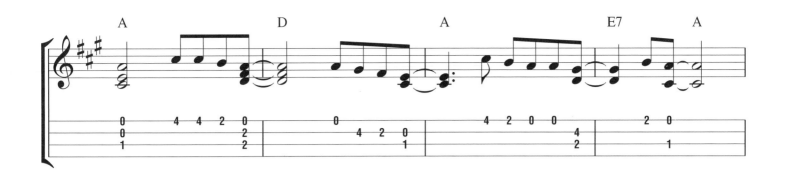

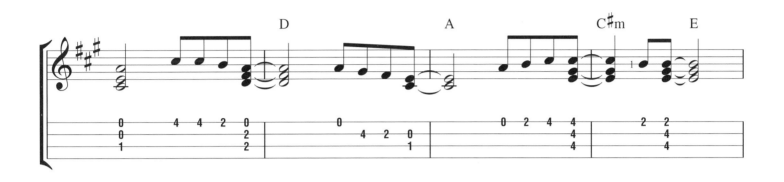

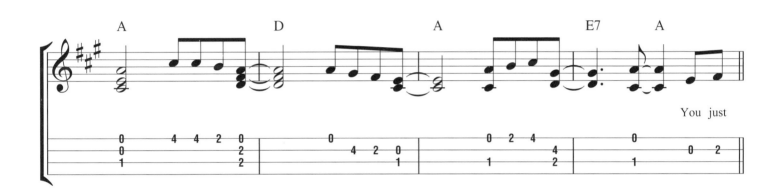

You just

C

call on me, bro-ther...

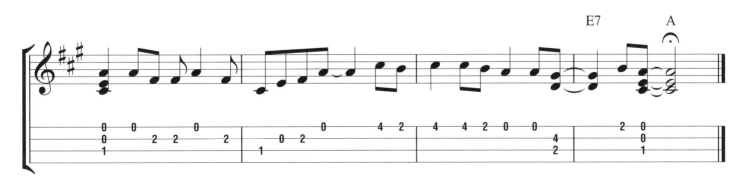

My Girl

Words and Music by Smokey Robinson and Ronald White

I've got sun - shine...

No Woman No Cry

Words and Music by Vincent Ford

No wom-an no cry...

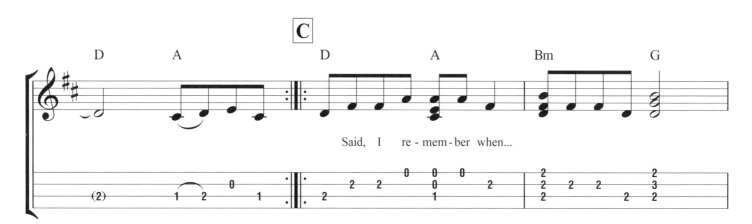

Said, I re-mem-ber when...

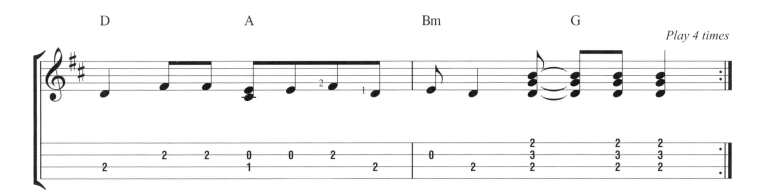

Play 4 times

D

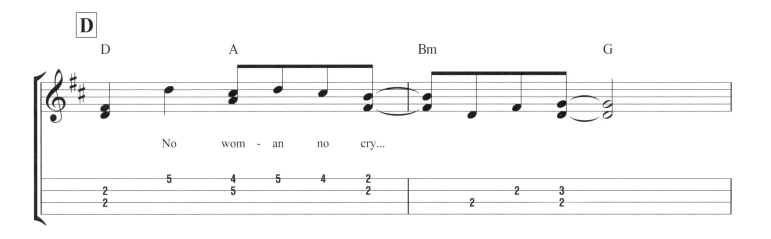

No wom - an no cry...

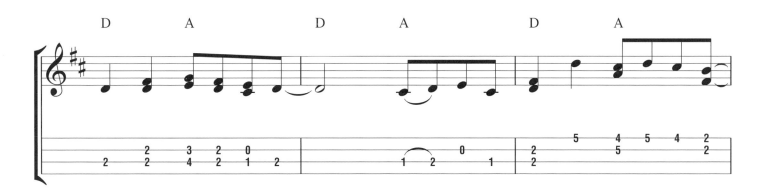

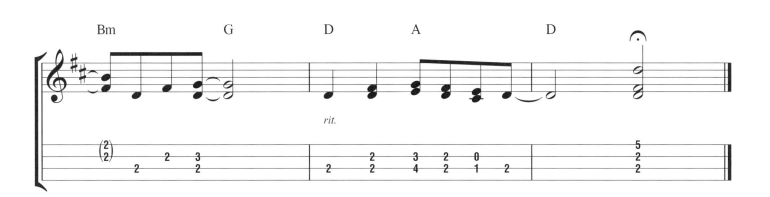

rit.

The Sound of Silence

Words and Music by Paul Simon

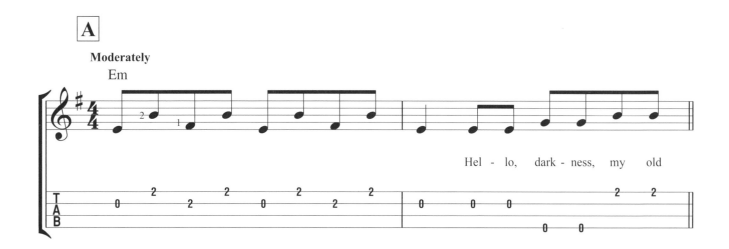

Hel - lo, dark - ness, my old

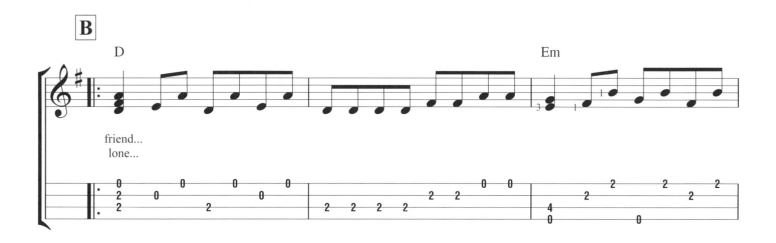

friend...
lone...

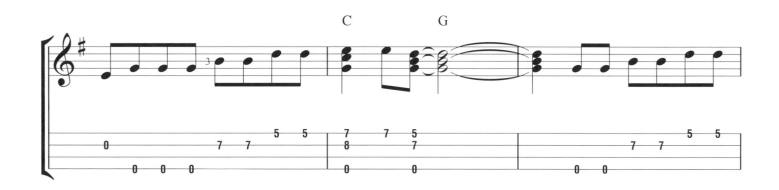

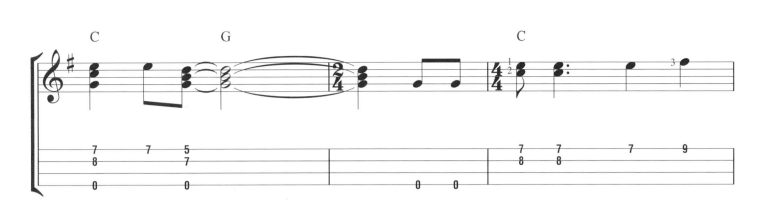

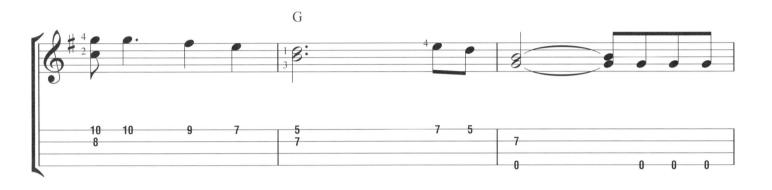

In rest - less dreams I walked a -

rit.

Stayin' Alive

from the Motion Picture SATURDAY NIGHT FEVER

Words and Music by Barry Gibb, Robin Gibb and Maurice Gibb

Moderately slow, in 2

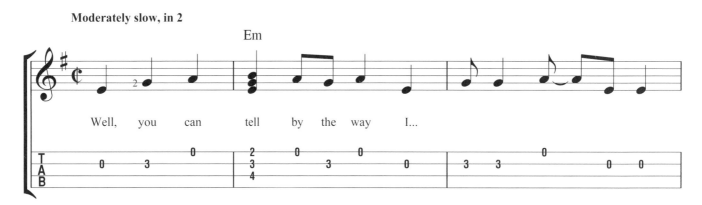

Well, you can tell by the way I...

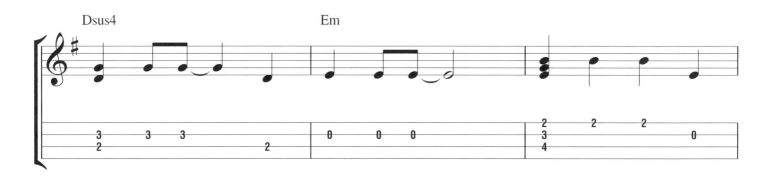

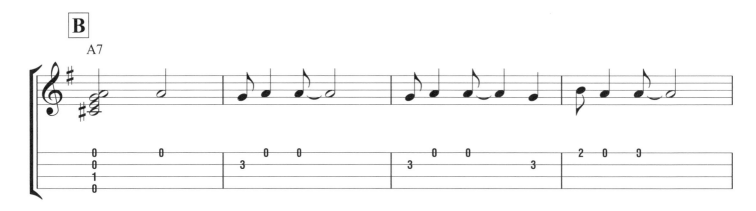

C

Em

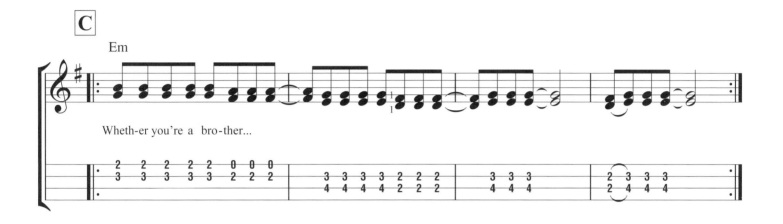

Wheth-er you're a bro-ther...

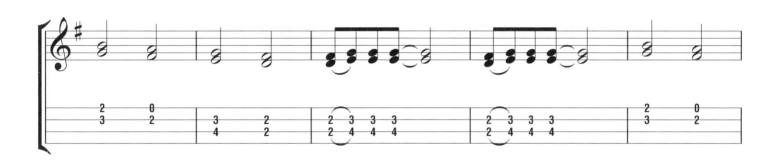

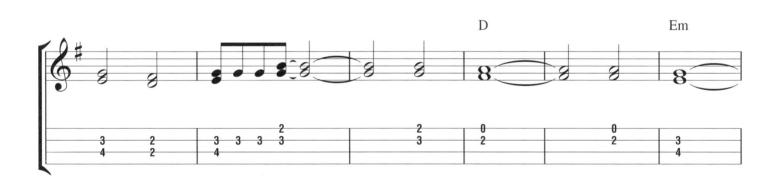

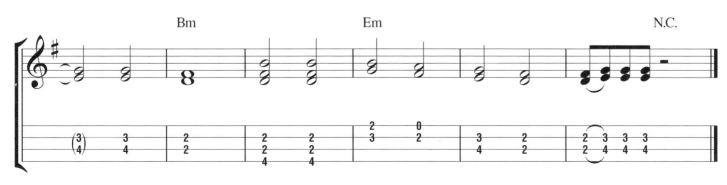

Sweet Child o' Mine

Words and Music by W. Axl Rose, Slash, Izzy Stradlin', Duff McKagan and Steven Adler

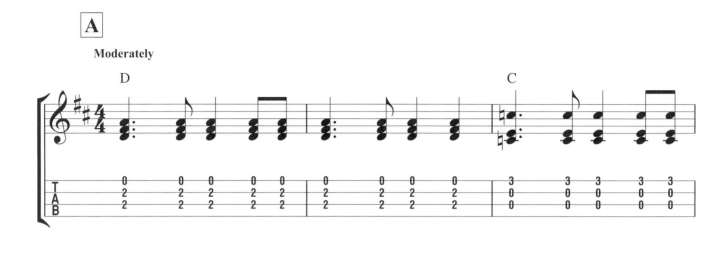

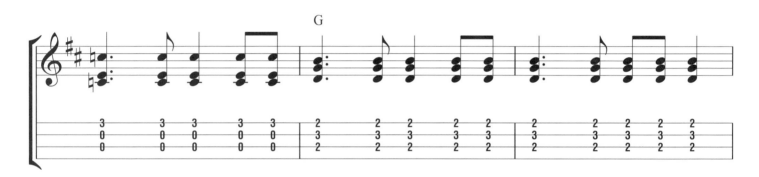

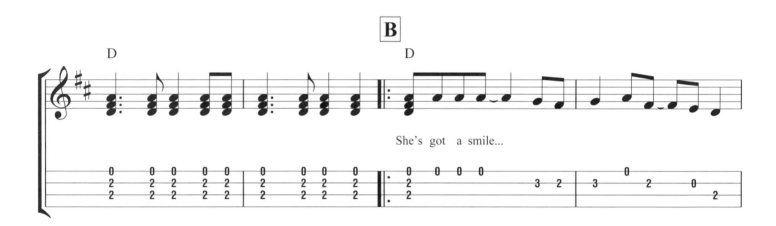

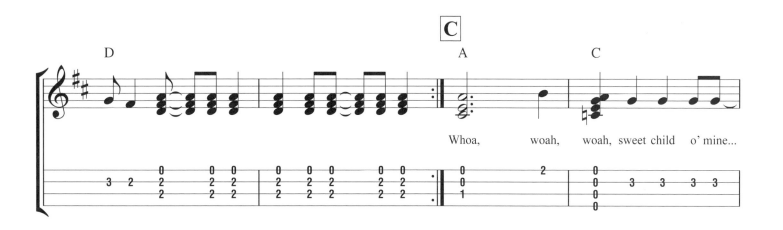

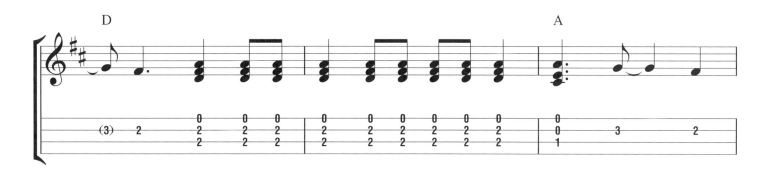

Whoa, woah, woah, sweet child o' mine...

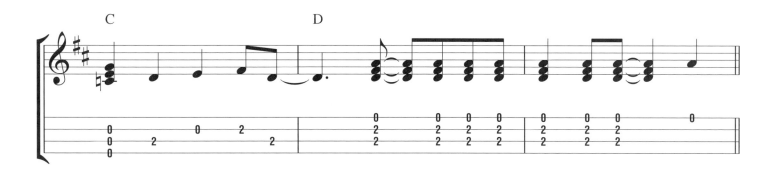

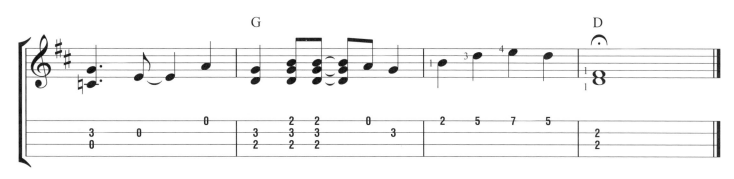

Tainted Love

Words and Music by Ed Cobb

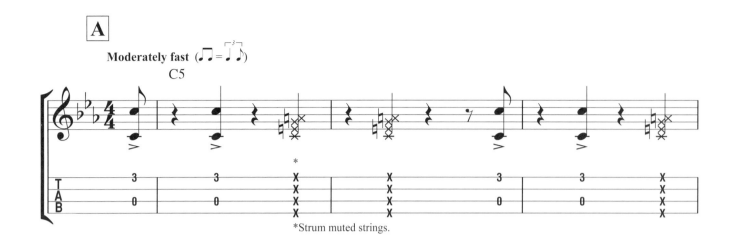

*Strum muted strings.

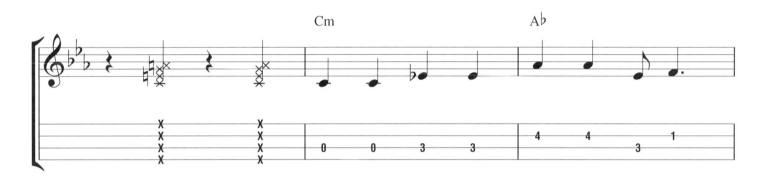

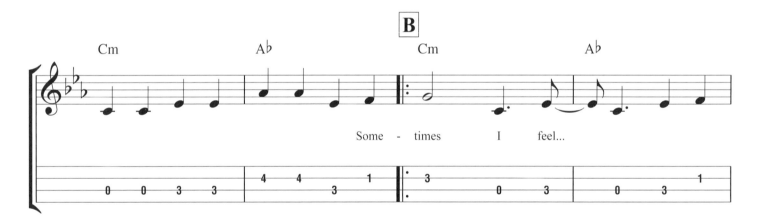

Some - times   I   feel...

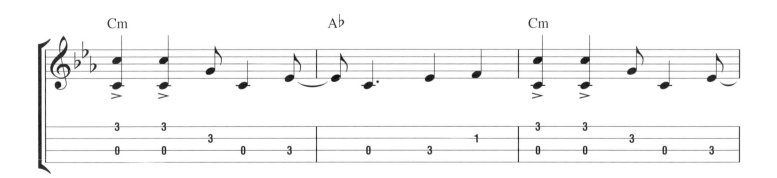

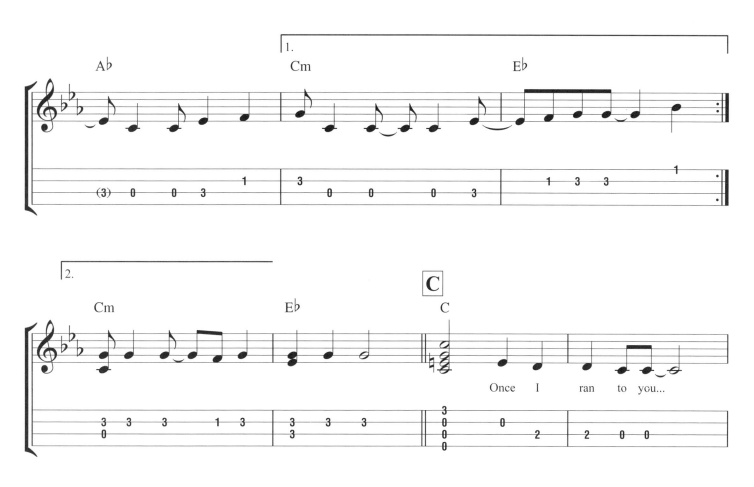

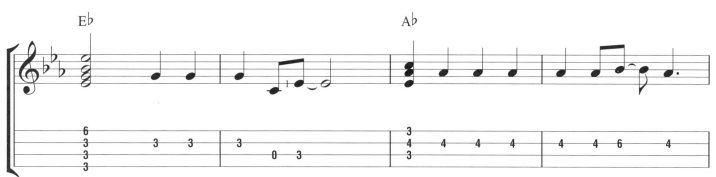

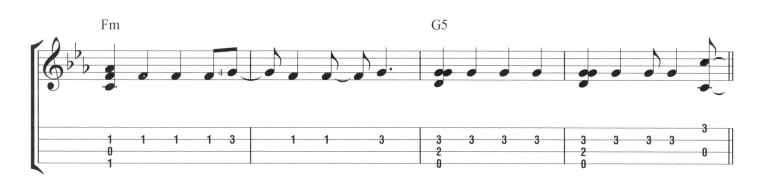

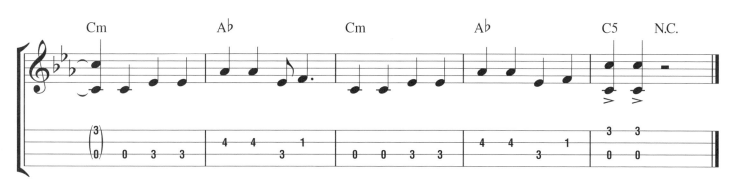

Time After Time

Words and Music by Cyndi Lauper and Rob Hyman

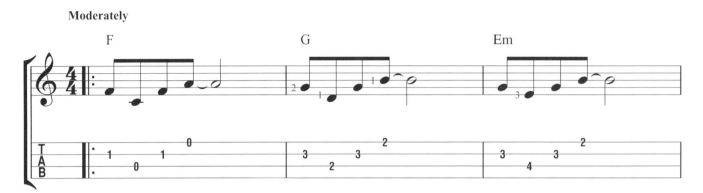

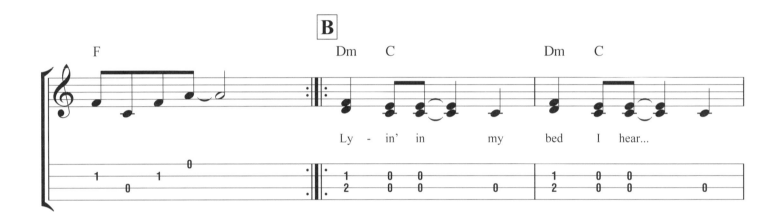

Ly - in' in   my   bed   I   hear...

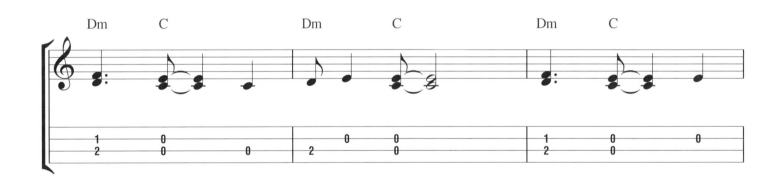

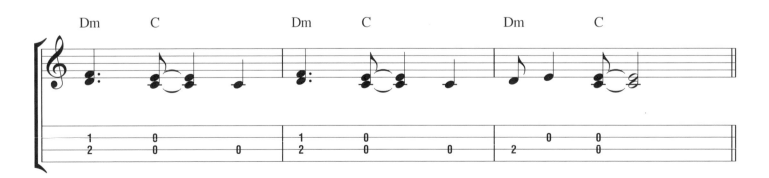

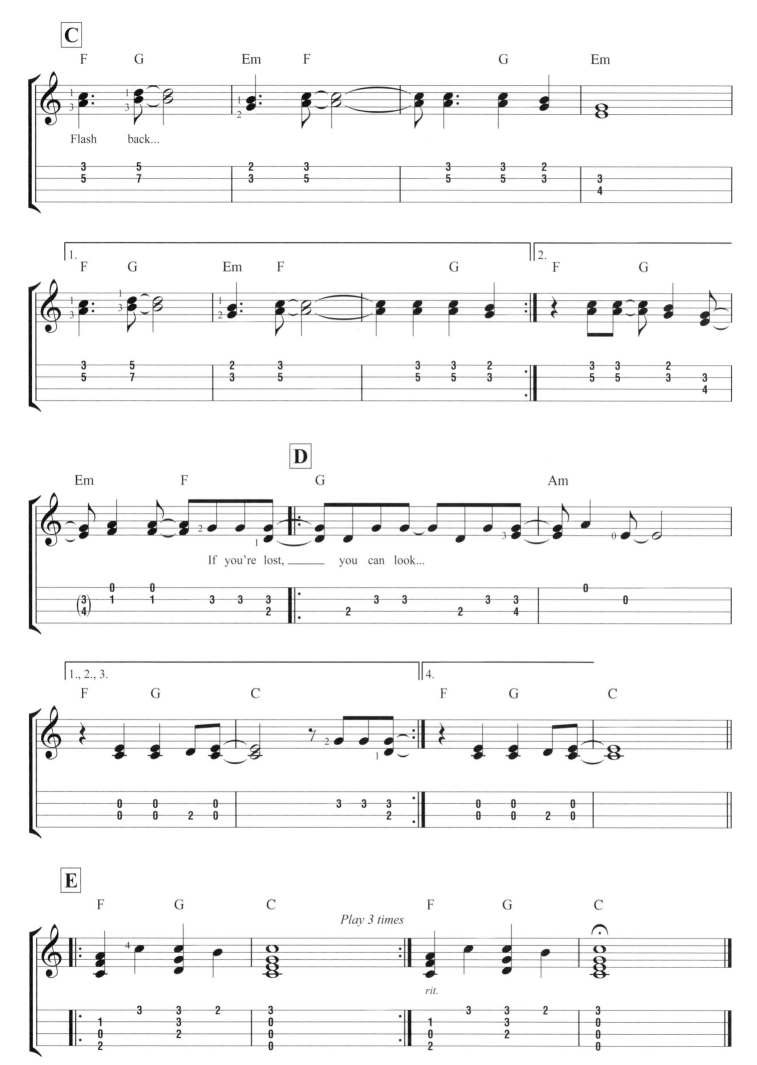

Y.M.C.A.

Words and Music by Jacques Morali, Henri Belolo and Victor Willis

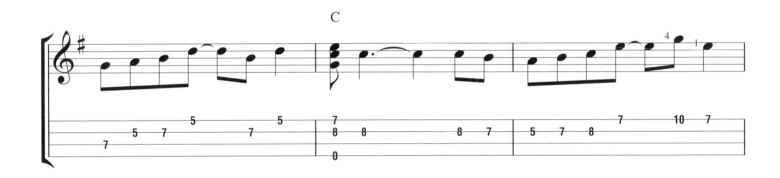

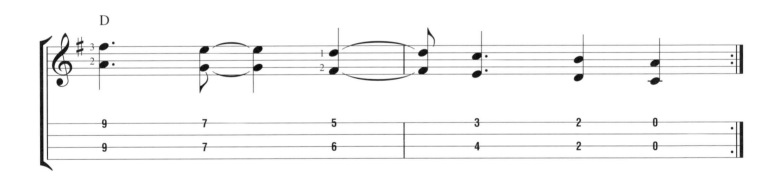

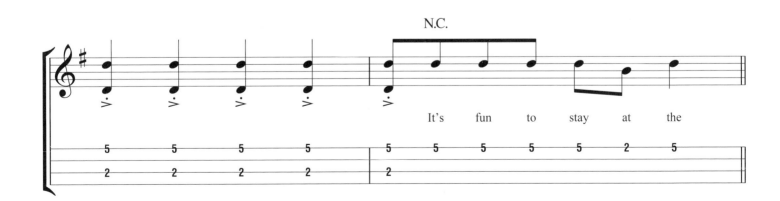

Wouldn't It Be Nice

Words and Music by Brian Wilson, Tony Asher and Mike Love

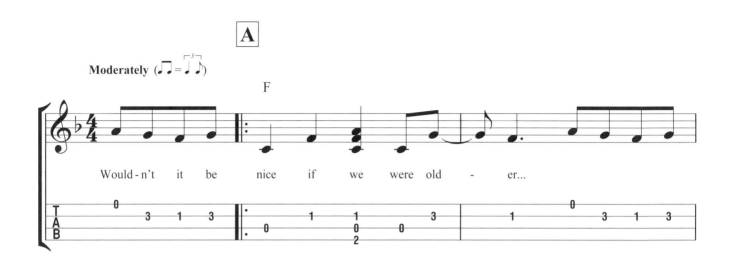

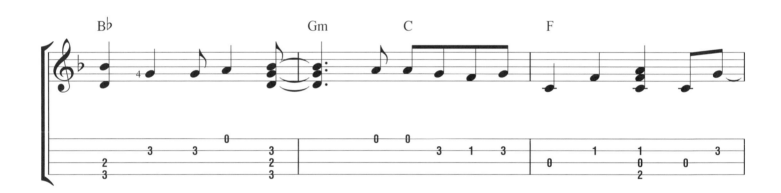

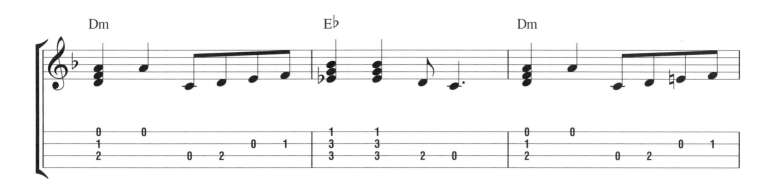

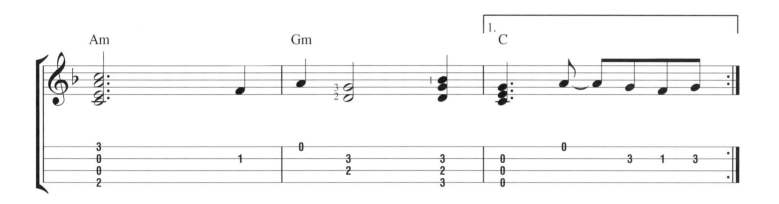

May - be   if   we...

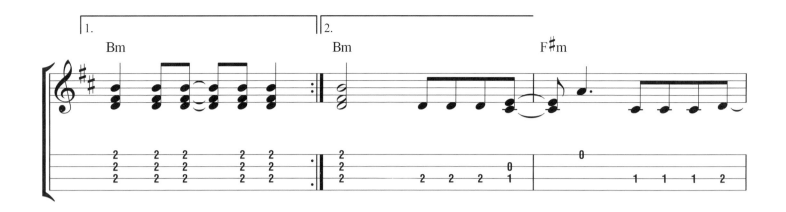

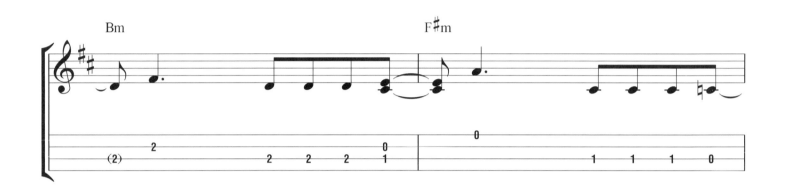

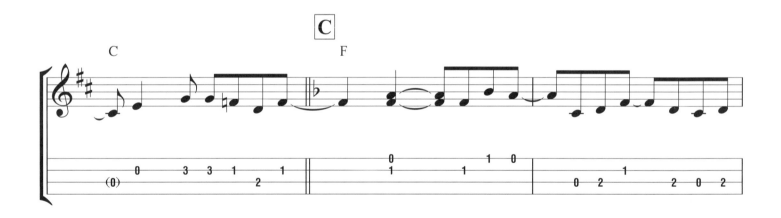

UKULELE NOTATION LEGEND

THE MUSICAL STAFF shows pitches and rhythms and is divided by bar lines into measures. Pitches are named after the first seven letters of the alphabet.

TABLATURE graphically represents the ukulele fingerboard. Each horizontal line represents a a string, and each number represents a fret.

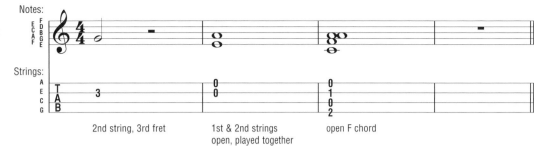

2nd string, 3rd fret | 1st & 2nd strings open, played together | open F chord

HALF-STEP BEND: Strike the note and bend up 1/2 step.

WHOLE-STEP BEND: Strike the note and bend up one step.

GRACE NOTE BEND: Strike the note and immediately bend up as indicated.

SLIGHT (MICROTONE) BEND: Strike the note and bend up 1/4 step.

BEND AND RELEASE: Strike the note and bend up as indicated, then release back to the original note. Only the first note is struck.

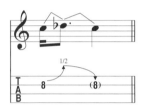

PRE-BEND: Bend the note as indicated, then strike it.

VIBRATO: The string is vibrated by rapidly bending and releasing the note with the fretting hand.

HAMMER-ON: Strike the first (lower) note with one finger, then sound the higher note (on the same string) with another finger by fretting it without picking.

PULL-OFF: Place both fingers on the notes to be sounded. Strike the first note and without picking, pull the finger off to sound the second (lower) note.

LEGATO SLIDE: Strike the first note and then slide the same fret-hand finger up or down to the second note. The second note is not struck.

SHIFT SLIDE: Same as legato slide, except the second note is struck.

TRILL: Very rapidly alternate between the notes indicated by continuously hammering on and pulling off.

TREMOLO PICKING: The note is picked as rapidly and continuously as possible.

NOTE: Tablature numbers in parentheses mean:

1. The note is being sustained over a system (note in standard notation is tied), or

2. The note is sustained, but a new articulation (such as a hammer-on, pull-off, slide or vibrato) begins, or

3. The note is a barely audible "ghost" note (note in standard notation is also in parentheses).

Additional Musical Definitions

 (accent)   • Accentuate note (play it louder)

 (staccato)   • Play the note short

D.S. al Coda   • Go back to the sign (𝄋), then play until the measure marked "***To Coda***," then skip to the section labelled "**Coda**."

D.C. al Fine   • Go back to the beginning of the song and play until the measure marked "***Fine***" (end).

N.C.   • No chord.

     • Repeat measures between signs.

   • When a repeated section has different endings, play the first ending only the first time and the second ending only the second time.

The Best Collections for Ukulele

The Best Songs Ever

70 songs have now been arranged for ukulele. Includes: Always • Bohemian Rhapsody • Memory • My Favorite Things • Over the Rainbow • Piano Man • What a Wonderful World • Yesterday • You Raise Me Up • and more.

00282413 . . . . $17.99

Campfire Songs for Ukulele

30 favorites to sing as you roast marshmallows and strum your uke around the campfire. Includes: God Bless the U.S.A. • Hallelujah • The House of the Rising Sun • I Walk the Line • Puff the Magic Dragon • Wagon Wheel • You Are My Sunshine • and more.

00129170 . . . . $14.99

The Daily Ukulele

compiled and arranged by
Liz and Jim Beloff
Strum a different song everyday with easy arrangements of 365 of your favorite songs in one big songbook! Includes favorites by the Beatles, Beach Boys, and Bob Dylan, folk songs, pop songs, kids' songs, Christmas carols, and Broadway and Hollywood tunes, all with a spiral binding for ease of use.

00240356 . . . . $39.99

The Daily Ukulele – Leap Year Edition

366 More Songs for Better Living
compiled and arranged by
Liz and Jim Beloff
An amazing second volume with 366 MORE songs for you to master each day of a leap year! Includes: Ain't No Sunshine • Calendar Girl • I Got You Babe • Lean on Me • Moondance • and many, many more.

00240681 . . . . $39.99

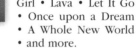

Disney Hits for Ukulele

Play 23 of your favorite Disney songs on your ukulele. Includes: The Bare Necessities • Cruella De Vil • Do You Want to Build a Snowman? • Kiss the Girl • Lava • Let It Go • Once upon a Dream • A Whole New World • and more.

00151250 . . . . $14.99

First 50 Songs You Should Play on Ukulele

An amazing collection of 50 accessible, must-know favorites: Edelweiss • Hey, Soul Sister • I Walk the Line • I'm Yours • Imagine • Over the Rainbow • Peaceful Easy Feeling • The Rainbow Connection • Riptide • and many more.

00149250 . . . . $14.99

The Ukulele 4 Chord Songbook

With just 4 chords, you can play 50 hot songs on your ukulele! Songs include: Brown Eyed Girl • Do Wah Diddy Diddy • Hey Ya! • Ho Hey • Jessie's Girl • Let It Be • One Love • Stand by Me • Toes • With or Without You • and many more.

00142050 . . . . $16.99

Simple Songs for Ukulele

50 favorites for standard G-C-E-A ukulele tuning, including: All Along the Watchtower • Can't Help Falling in Love • Don't Worry, Be Happy • Ho Hey • I'm Yours • King of the Road • Sweet Home Alabama • You Are My Sunshine • and more.

00156815 . . . . $14.99

Top Hits of 2019

Strum your favorite songs of 2019 on the uke. Includes: Bad Guy (Billie Eilish) • I Don't Care (Ed Sheeran & Justin Bieber) • ME! (Taylor Swift) • Old Town Road (Remix) (Lil Nas X feat. Billy Ray Cyrus) • Senorita (Shawn Mendes & Camila Cabello) • Someone You Loved (Lewis Capaldi) • and more.

00302274 . . . . $14.99

The Ukulele 3 Chord Songbook

If you know three chords, you can play these 50 great hits! Songs include: Bad Moon Rising • A Boy Named Sue • King of the Road • Leaving on a Jet Plane • Shelter from the Storm • Time for Me to Fly • Twist and Shout • and many more.

00141143 . . . . $16.99

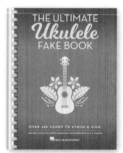

The Ultimate Ukulele Fake Book

Uke enthusiasts will love this giant, spiral-bound collection of over 400 songs for uke! Includes: Crazy • Dancing Queen • Downtown • Fields of Gold • Happy • Hey Jude • 7 Years • Summertime • Thinking Out Loud • Thriller • Wagon Wheel • and more.

00175500 . . . . $45.00

Ukulele – The Most Requested Songs

Strum & Sing Series
Cherry Lane Music
Nearly 50 favorites all expertly arranged for ukulele! Includes: Bubbly • Build Me Up, Buttercup • Cecilia • Georgia on My Mind • Kokomo • L-O-V-E • Your Body Is a Wonderland • and dozens more.

02501453 . . . . $14.99

HAL•LEONARD®

Prices, contents, and availability subject to change.